YOUR DAILY DOSE OF BUSINESS WOMANS CONFIDENCE AND SUCCESS

Proven ways to increase sales, confidence and success in 2 minutes a day

Mandie Holgate

WHY PEOPLE LOVE THIS BOOK AND MANDIE'S WORDS OF WISDOM:

"Mandie has been a life saver when it comes to getting the right mindset for business. She has a wonderful way of deciphering what's going on in someone's head and bringing out the positives and fighting the negatives. I thoroughly enjoy working with her and look forward to it continuing - onward and upward!"

Isobel Chaplin, IJC Finance Ltd.

"Officially I know this book is meant for women, and yes I did get a few funny looks reading this on the Tube, however as a business man I found this book very very useful, and while "wearing heels, or my favourite dress" was not directly right for me, the idea about about wearing my best was just as relevant, brilliant read."

Nick Looby, Feet On The Ground Events.

'I am impressed with Mandie's knowledge, practical experience and delivery style. She is an inspirational and dynamic business mentor and coach with incredible energy and a sense of fun. As testimony to our belief in Mandie's ability, she has been selected as one of experts to deliver workshops for our current business engagement project.'

Kae Skinner, Anglia Ruskin University, Med Tech Programme.

'Mandie's energy and enthusiasm is infectious and inspirational. Her passion for supporting and developing others is reinforced through her understanding and experience. She recognises the challenges facing modern day businesses and works with empathy and drive to enable people to rise to those challenges to improve the chances of their success.'

Lesley Cresswell, Director of Learning and Sustainability Education and Training Academy.

'Mandie is one of the most inspiring women that I have met. She is passionate about helping others.'

Stella Bradbrook Editor, About My Area

"I started my own business this year and met Mandie Holgate. She has been so inspirational to my business I brought her book and found it amazing, its a daily dose of inspiration, top tips and its like she is standing besides you giving the advice. I am not a reader, but this book is always with me and I read a bit every day. Can't recommend this highly enough"

Julie Blanche - The Bra Consultancy

WHAT DO YOU WANT?

Can I guess what you want?
If you are a business woman it's highly likely you are not just a business woman. You're a hard working, incredibly busy woman that happens to be passionate about your career as well as probably a million other things, whether that's kids, partners, pets, charities, hobbies or lovers (Ok so I've only suggested a few!)

How do you create the time to go for your ambitions, goals and aspirations?

Where do you create the space to be a woman that loves the life she is living?

How do you know you are on the right track?

What can you do when you feel like the delicate balance of your life is about to come crashing down around your ears?

Where can you get simple easy to action ideas to increase your success levels and feel like you are in control of your life?

You may be thinking that you need to add more skills to your repertoire, but since you hardly have time to leave the house looking great and cramming everything else in that needs doing, when are you going to have the time or the energy to add essential 21st Century business women skills to your Skill and mind set?

There's a million books telling you how to run the most successful business, have happy kids and relationships, look good, feel good, be more confident, be a great public speaker, climb the ladder to success, cook, make more money, and even be a super saver

– but when time is the most precious commodity you own, all you want is a sentence from someone that gives a dam about your success, to lay in the subconscious of your busy mind to get you started, and this book will do just that.

No need to read the same sentence again and again because you are so shattered and you realise that you've not paid a word of attention to what you've just read because you were mentally planning your next day.

No more never finishing the paragraph, let alone the book, because your brain is whirring with a million jobs.

No more guilt tripping every time you walk past the book shelf, because you read the first chapter and then it is sat there gathering dust with the other books that could change your life.

HOW TO READ
THIS BOOK

Just pick this book up once a day and read that one sentence. It will share with you a little idea to help you be more organised, more confident, more successful, or even get a big fat smile on your face (that's genuine for a change and not the "Oh no, I've got to look like I'm holding this all together!")

This booked is based on years of working with business women who wanted to take their business to the next level, a ton of science and research and a lot of passion for your success.

But basically this book is jammed packed with ideas to help you be the best version of you.

You on a good day.

In control.

Getting results.

Loving your life and having a ball!

No long paragraphs, just short snappy sentences rammed full of highly successful ways to make it all work for you.

Its 3 minutes of your day that will help you get more out of your life. Now you really deserve that so let's go.

(A word of advice to ensure this really could help you.)Much of 21st Century life is made to give us more time and an easier life, however we've never been so stressed and over worked. Just like the email you open but don't action, this book is here to help your life, but only if you use it correctly.

Thus only open this book if you have the 3 minutes to read that sentence and work out how you intend to action it.

Only open this book if you feel you have the spare 180 seconds to actually take action, otherwise all you have done is add another thought into your ridiculously busy mind.)

LET'S DO THIS...

1. If you wrote a wish list of things you would love to see happen, what would be on there? If you don't write it down how can you be working towards it? Would you jump in your car and drive to the other end of the country without checking the basics?

Get's you thinking doesn't it?

2. When you are up against it, when there are 400 jobs all needing your attention. STOP.

Now prioritise. Unless you turned into a robot over night all you are going to do is stress yourself out, not achieve as much as you want and have a lousy day.

So prioritise.

Be realistic in what you can achieve, and get going.

3. Confidence comes from within, are you allowing external forces to dictate whether you are happy with your performance or not? Ensure you know in your heart that you are the best. That you deserve to succeed and it is going to happen.

4. Don't sweat the small stuff. Concentrate on what makes the difference to your daily success. And besides sweat looks awful on your great outfit.

5. Before you start tapping on that keyboard ask yourself "would I get a better result from picking up the phone and talking to this person?"

It works wonders on your daily success.

6. What is your favourite way to be motivated? It's good to know for the tough days and will help you get back on track faster.

7. Networking can be a very powerful part of your strategy to get the results in your business and your life. You never know who knows who. However, it is not the only thing you need to do to ensure you get where you want to go. Ask yourself what follow up do you need to do?

8. Do you know the numbers?

How much did you earn and spend this week, this month?

What impact could that knowledge have on your strategy for the coming week, month and year?

Planning for the future may sound dull, but visualising that dream pad, new car or the feel of that tropical sun on your back isn't!

9. Do you know the value of your time? The next time you spend time doing something, think of it as spending a £1 a minute. Would you be more careful with your time?

If you don't value your time, why should anyone else?

10. Having a bad day?

A Bad week?

Make the choice that from this second on what has happened is in the past and the here and now and the future are the place to target your focus. So what are you choosing to focus on? And how will that impact on your day or your success?

11. Make 2 lists.

1. "Things that have to be done"

2. "Things that you would love to do"

Include things like "be a confident public speaker", "fly to Oz", "clear that pile of paperwork from the edge of my desk", etc.

And concentrate only on achieving the first one on each list. Don't look at another until it's done and gone. Starting small can be the incentive to grow your goals ambitiously.

Could that work for you?

Or would it suit your style to aim for the stars?

12. When it comes to Social Media do you talk to other people or just talk at the online world? How effective would that be in a roomful of people?

Get involved, ask questions, add your thoughts – and be nice!

And remember what you post today can be seen forever, and you never know whose reading!

Ever had Stephen Fry say you're a good writer? I have......you just never know whose reading!

13. Ever attended a seminar or a workshop?

Ever read a business development or personal development book?

How much did you put into action?

Think about this for a moment, do you know how much money was spent on self help books last year? If every person put all that into action how amazing would that be? If you were to put one thing you read or heard into action what would that be? And what impact could that have on your personal and professional life? Don't just read this do something about it. You are so worth it!

14. Every conversation and interaction needs to end with a win

win situation. You never know when you may need that person and who they might know.

15. Everybody no matter how annoying, obnoxious, frustrating or just plain mean they are to you today, remember this, and it's a difficult one......Everyone is doing their best. Their best takes into account their negative beliefs, values and experiences to date, that have accumulated in making them the person they are today. You don't suddenly have to love the company of the most annoying person on the planet, but it does give you an insight as to why they are living the life they are leading.

16. When things get tough, getting stressed won't fix it and worrying about what went wrong is not your primary concern, putting it right is. So concentrate on what CAN be achieved, prioritise and then think about WHAT you could learn from it.

17. Nobody has endless good days do they?

But how great would that be?

But you're thinking how unrealistic is that! Well on those days were the rain is horizontal, the car won't start, the cats been sick and your email is down.

Smile – frowning won't fix any of it, but smiling will set off those endorphins. Now do you fancy tackling a tough day alone or with a few endorphins helping you along?

18. Public speaking can be scary (for everyone) it is the beliefs you hold about your ability to deliver and the confidence you hold in yourself that will help you shine.

So ask yourself do you believe in your ability to deliver, if not what do you need to do?

And what can you do to feel confident – and remember, it is not stage fright it is nervous energy. Performance energy that you can use to be awesome in front of your audience.

19. What are you putting up with?

Step out of your life for a moment, and ask yourself what have you decided to put up with?
And what impact is that having on your success?

20. If you are looking for motivation, think about a great day, a great turnout, a great contract you gained or a personal achievement and really think about the feelings you went through. The happiness, the pride, the joy, the elation and hang on to that all day long and watch yourself go like a squirrel on rocket fuel!

21. Nervous about walking into a room full of people or a new environment?

Before you walk in the room, concentrate on the way you want to feel as you head home with 5 great new contacts from that networking event (remember it's not about collecting 100's, it's about building great relationships) or with the next meeting booked or the contract signed. Program your brain's Sat Nav to see, feel and sense the result you want. You can do it.

22. Personal life does exist and you are human. If you don't allow time for life outside of work, somewhere down the road you are in for a rough ride. Always care for your health and personal life as much as you do your professional. Do you set personal goals like you do business ones?

Does your schedule include personal appointments for pleasure as well as a busy business woman's' life?

23. Achieving your goals starts with a very clear goal. Is your goal so clear you can practically reach out and touch it?

24. You know when you have those great days that make you beam from ear to ear?

Guess what, I believe you are capable of having even more of them. Go for it!

25. What don't you know?

There is nothing wrong with putting your hand up and saying I don't know the answer to this. But there is a problem in not dealing with it. Learn and progress.

If you don't you are allowing it to be an obstacle to your success.

Now who wants that?

26. You are up to your eyes in a million jobs. Deadlines are everywhere. Customers are breathing down your neck. You don't feel like you have time to think. So would you say that's the worst time ever to consider walking away from all that work for one whole hour and to self indulge in something that makes you feel special, pampered, relaxed, calm and happy? Wrong.

Creating a bit of "Me Time" allows your brain to process everything that is going on, makes you calmer and more capable of dealing with high stress, high octane situations and that leads to more success. So what are you going to plan?

27. If you are easily distracted or face a task you dread today. What will motivate you to get on with it?

And does it just come down to D.I.N?

Do It Now.

Think how great you will feel when that task is gone from your day?

And always remember the initials D.I.N to power you up for action.

28. How are you feeling today?

If you are not feeling like you are the best at what you do. What impact will that have on your day?

Your work?

Your life?

I believe you are amazing so get out there and be the amazing business women you know you are. It's not arrogance, its inner confidence that says whatever comes my way.... bring it on.

29. If in doubt leave it out. (Short sweet and it works a treat.)

30. Remove these words from your vocabulary;

Try, Should, Can't and Might.

They are adding guilt and blame to your life and who needs that?

Guess what words can take their place?

31. Know when to work really hard, when to walk away and do something different, when to take a break, when to listen, when not to listen – basically learn to listen to you. To what is most essential every minute of every day to your success. Your subconscious amasses tons of information, allow it to help you.

32. Your answers will not always be in front a screen. Who may you need to speak to?

Who could help?

Where else could you turn?

Are your nearest and dearest really the best people to get advice for your professional success from?

If not, who is?

33. Lists are only any good if there are tangible things on there that you work at achieving. Stop adding the easy stuff and ignoring the tough jobs. Tick off the toughest job today and guess how amazing it will feel.

34. Did you run in the office turn on the lap top and start piling through the emails.

Great right?

WRONG. Before you do anything every day of your working life, your first job is to ascertain what are the priorities for the day.

What needs to be done?

What am I putting off?

What could I leave to another day, but I chose not to because this is easier?

35. If you don't understand what someone does for a living...ask.

If you choose not to ask, how are you going to effectively connect someone to the right kinds of people?

Another idea to power up your networking and boost your success.

36. When was the last time you contacted your existing customers to make them feel special. If you don't guess what, your competitors will! This goes for contacts and business associates too, keeping in touch keeps you in their thoughts.

And you don't want your fabulousness to be forgotten do you?

37. When the going gets tough, give up. Right?

No, of course not.

Access the situation without emotion.

What do you need to learn from this experience?

What could you do differently?

Who could you talk to?

What do you need to ask yourself?

38. What are your competitors up to?

What's going on in your industry?

It is essential that you know what else is available to your customers and potential new customers and you do that by research. If you were buying what you offer, do you stand out as the best?

If you were to search for what you do online do you shine?

Exactly the same applies if you are employed. Are you shining brightly as the next potential member of the board?

39. When was the last time you respected your body?

If your friend worked as hard as you do without breaks, what would you say to them? If you don't respect your body and give it what it needs just like your success, eventually the body will demand a stop (and you may not get a say on when that is!)

40. Trust your gut instinct – if something feels wrong. Sleep on it.

41. Do you have a glass of water at your desk, in your office, in the car (okay so maybe a bottle of water there!) dehydrated brains are not happy effective brains.

42. Is social media a powerful tool in your marketing strategy or is it a tool of procrastination?

You should have a plan for social media just like you need for every other area of your marketing strategy, just as you do for many other areas of your business and life. Otherwise it will be an unwanted distraction – get smart and use Hootsuite or Tweet-Deck today – Google it and get started. And new tools are coming on the market all the time. Keep up to date and see how they could be making your time work better.

43. Are you lacking in confidence in an area of your business or your life?

If you are you're allowing that to be an obstacle to your success. Now who wants one of those?

You deserve to be the best at what you do so deal with that confidence issue today.

If it all feels too much who could help you? What could help you?

What could work for you?

Music, photos of happy times, memories, sentimental jewellery, Notes in prominent places reinforcing your confidence are a few ideas to get you started.

44. When was the last time you congratulated yourself, your business and your team for your success and triumphs?

We so often concentrate on the negative, on what we have not achieved. On how we failed. So today take a moment to really appreciate all that you have achieved. It really can create momentum and motivation to achieve even more and keep you aiming for the goals that you really want in life.

45. You know how when you listen to someone else talk about their problems you feel like you know the best course of action and you are full of great ideas and yet when it comes to your own issues and your obstacles you hit a blank? Why not try brainstorming with a friend or take a step back and ask yourself what would I tell someone else to do?

46. Every distraction you allow to take your attention away from the job at hand will ensure it takes an average of 15 minutes to get back into the flow of working. So if you look at just 3 emails an hour that is an additional 45 minutes you could be adding to that task. Get in the flow, turn the email off and get on with it.

47. Are you really busy? But are you really busy with the stuff that grows your business or with the day to day stuff that just has to be done? Yes the day to day stuff has to be done but if you don't factor in time to grow your business, achieve your goals and get what you want, it will be stuck the way it is today, forever.

48. Are you using social media for your business?

It is a great tool for business. Getting known as the expert, growing your network, reinforcing those great relationships, learning new ideas, finding out about events and so much more – and its free.

Don't you just love free stuff that is great for your business?

49. What does your office space look like?

Is it a productive environment that enthuses you?

Does it give you motivation and inspiration the minute you walk in?

Do you feel your office ensures you are at your most productive?

If not what do you need to do?

If your work space sparkles and says volumes about you, what could that do for your positivity and for taking action?

50. You know you are giving the best possible service to your customers. But are you getting the best possible service from your suppliers? Are you getting a good fair price that allows you and

your suppliers to grow, or have you slipped into a relationship because it was easy, that does not really deliver what your business needs? Always take the time to ensure you are getting the service, standard and results from your suppliers that your customers can expect from you.

51. When you look in the mirror as you leave the house, do you think "Wow I'm looking gorgeous!" or do you instantly start listing your faults?

Do you wonder what that does for your confidence?

Think about what that might do for your mindset as you leave the house?

Would you do that to your best friend?

52. Go for it! Stop researching and preparing and just do it. You can do it, it will be great, you will be amazing and everyone will love it and you. Stop putting obstacles in the way and go for it!

53. When it gets to about an hour before you are going to stop work for the day, take a moment to step away from what you are doing and consciously decide if you are on target to achieve what you set out to achieve today. What can you do to ensure you finish work today feeling like real progress, success and productivity happened today?

54. Newsletters, email marketing, social media are only any good if they are working to drive customers to your door and getting you the success you want.

Can you say where your customers came from? Where they found you?

What made them connect?

Knowing this information can be the key to getting even more.

55. What goals have you set for this year?

And how are they going?

Are you on target to achieve them?

Do you need to reassess your goals?

Are they realistic?

Will they take your business, your life, and your success to where you want to be in 6 months or a year's time?

Did you just read this and let the words wash over you to be forgotten, or will you actually take a few moments today to actually answer these questions?

What could that do for your success?

56. 1, 2, 3, 4, 5 counting is easy. So is everything else if you practice it enough. Will that get you thinking today about what you need to practice more?

57. Free is not always the best for business. Giving away free stuff can be great but think it through, what results do you expect to receive from it?

What is the genuine cost to you when you include, time, effort and the other things you could have been doing to deliver success to your door?

How will you monitor the level of results it creates?

58. Did you know you are capable of achieving amazing things?

Did you know you can achieve anything you want to?

Did you know many of the people that surround you right now think you are amazing? Did you know that I absolutely believe that anything you want to achieve you can?

It's a thought to pop into your head right?

59. When it comes to your accounts however much you hate number crunching, you have got to know them. So what numbers do you need to know? If you are still cringing at the thought, ask yourself how you would feel if your numbers weren't adding up and you were missing out. Does that make you cringe more?

60. "If you can't explain something simply you don't understand it" Well, that's the kind of thing Einstein said. So can you succinctly tell someone how fabulous your business is?

Why you are the right woman for them?

Can you get the message across about why you and not the next person. Remember, keep it simple.

61. Wouldn't it be nice if you could read your potential customers minds?

Answer the questions they don't feel comfortable asking?

Truly understanding your customers enables you to communicate more effectively with them. Anonymous surveys could help. That or a course in telepathy.

62. Ever felt like giving up?

Don't worry everyone has.

What do you need to remember to get you through those tough days?

Who can you rely on to pick you up and help you remember how amazing you are?

Is there a song that makes you smile every time?

An outfit that makes you feel amazing?

Give the tough days the what for. Remember you're brilliant.

63. What's on the agenda for today?

Do the worst job first and reward yourself for doing it. If you hate phone calls and love social media, set yourself the target of dealing with 5 phone calls and reward yourself with 20 minutes social media time. Have to do some number crunching and hate it? Reward yourself when it's done with your favourite sweet treat or coffee fix and five minutes time out.

You get the picture.

64. If you are not prepared to make mistakes in life, you are missing out on living. Yes making mistakes can hurt, be embarrassing and costly in more than just financial ways, but mistakes bring learning, ideas and opportunities so be prepared to fail once in a while – You never know where it might lead. Chocolate chip cookies were invented by mistake!

65. Do you give a call to action in your marketing? Is it obvious?

Are there contact details in your email signature?

Don't make your potential customers work too hard to get in touch with you.

66. Clear goals laid out for the day?

Do you know what the objectives are for the week?

Does everyone that it could impact on know the same information that you do?

Is your team up to speed too and I'm not just talking about the people you work with all day. What about the people that matter the most to you, planned them into your busy schedule?

67. Waiting for someone at a meeting?

A smart phone can be your time saving business boosting tool.

Send a useful tweet to your followers, reply to someone else's post. Answer just one email or phone call and it could make your return to the office easier.

68. When a busy woman walks into the room, you know she is capable of achieving all she sets her mind to. The way she walks, the way she carries herself, it all says I can do it, this will work.

What does your walk say about you?

Shoulders back?

Full of pride?

Ready for anything?

69. Remember those 2 lists I asked you to come up with?

Well how is it going?

Did you write them out and now are they hidden under a mountain of work or are you sticking to them?

If you stick with it, those lists will spur on motivation and continued success, now don't you deserve that?

70. Whether you work for an international corporation a local store or you are a sole trader, you need this.

What is it?

Tell you tomorrow, anticipation can be a good thing – for today keep being brilliant.

71. Remember yesterday's question?

The answer is you need inner belief that you are doing the right thing, that you are in the right place, setting out to achieve the right things. Do you not feel like that?

Maybe you need some space today to think about what really matters to you and your success. Just a thought.

72. Do you need to learn some new skills to be good at that job you hate?

Or is it just a case of doing it more often to become confident?

When you understand the reason for your lack of action, it can power you into action.

73. Today come up with a list of everything you think a woman needs for success. Every attribute, belief, experience, skill, attitude and anything else you can think of. Tell you more tomorrow...

74. What was on your list of what a woman needs for success?

I wonder if at the top of the list was to know your finances inside out?

No?

But it's absolutely essential that you know how much you have got, how much you need, how much you want and how you are going to get it. Do you have those answers?

And did the list of what a woman needs for success get you thinking?

75. Is the sun shining?

Are the birds singing?

Does every traffic light turn green as you reach them?

Are you wearing your favourite outfit, looking amazing?

Funny how things on the outside create something on the inside isn't it?

What would it take to feel that inner happiness as you step out the door this morning?

That feeling that whatever happens I can handle it AND have a great day.

76. If you were to list 5 wishes that were to happen to you this year, what would be on that list?

Would you say that you are doing all you can to get what you deserve and want in life?

77. "If you don't ask you don't get" as my Mum used to say. Same goes for business. So pluck up the courage and ask away.

What's the worst that could happen?

Right, now get that out of your head and concentrate on what you want to happen, because it's far more likely to.

Go for it!

78. It's a little known fact that being brilliant comes naturally to everyone. When you were a baby nobody sat you down and said "Right in the next 5 years I want you to learn to walk, talk, read, write, dress yourself, interact and use a grown up toilet." Children just naturally learn how to be the best version of a child.

So naturally be brilliant. Naturally allow that brilliance to shine through every day. You've been doing it since birth!

79. When it comes to that job on the corner of your desk that you have been ignoring for weeks, stop it!

Leaving it to Ron never works.... Who's Ron? "Later Ron." He's lazy. He never gets the job done and you just can't rely on him, now YOU on the other hand, I would rely on you every time.

80. When was the last time you said a hello to your customers and really useful contacts?

Not trying to sell them anything, not wanting or needing anything, not hoping you might find them in the mood to buy or ready to tell everyone how great you are, just got on the phone (checked it was a good time to talk – always good to be considerate right?) and said, "how's things" "Thought I would see if there was anything we needed to be aware of", kind of call. It works wonders for keeping on people's radars.

(For all the right reasons.)

81. Some days you just wake up feeling like it's going to be a tough day right?

Day's like that you need a bit of motivation. Crank up the radio, take time to make fresh coffee, polish your nails, or have a bath instead of a shower. Treat yourself right from the minute you get up and you will respect yourself more – well you are worth it!

82. Tweeting? Loving LinkedIn? Facebook fabulous? Instagram Influencer? Working for business? Do you check to see if your links get followed, and for how long, by whom, and at what time of day? If you don't know how to do things like this then you are missing out on great info, that will help you interact with your ideal clients, when they would most like to. And that can lead to interactive, engagement, leads and best of all sales!

83. It is not what happens in business that is the problem; it's the way that you choose to handle it. Notice I say the way you "choose" because you can choose to deal with things any way you wish. So can they help rocket your success or hold you back?

84. If you could do one thing today differently what would that be?

What impact could that have on your business?

On your success?

Small changes can have a big impact on your results.

85. Okay so not wanting to sound like your mum here, but have you had a decent breakfast?

Did you get enough sleep?

Do you feel refreshed and ready for action? Guess what, if you don't, then that will impact on your performance today. Just Google the importance of being hydrated by that stuff that comes out of your taps!

86. If you put nothing in, you get nothing out. Well I do love little nuggets of useful thoughts for the day. What could you do with this one? Would you say you give everything 100%?

And by the way if you can't give 100% to something is it time to outsource that one?

Get some advice?

Or learn some new skills?

87. A smile on your face when you start the day could work wonders. This is not some girly bunkum here, it's a fact. Even if you are not feeling like the happiest bunny on the planet, a fake or real smile still releases endorphins and guess what?

The more you smile, the better you will feel. Grin and bear it has never felt so good.

88. Sometimes the very thought of a job is enough to put you off, but ask yourself "why?" What is it that is putting that level of dread and fear into it?

Ask yourself do you need to learn something new, believe in yourself or raise your confidence levels?

Knowing why you fear something can work a treat. And sometimes it just comes down to doing it.

So which is it?

89. Whether you are redesigning your website, taking over the world, pitching to your perfect client, baking a cake, hugging, banking, or reading a book. LIVE IN THE MOMENT. If you are constantly thinking over your shoulder to the next task, you will always be missing out. Missing out on space, creativity, time, quietness, relaxation, laughter, concentration, ideas, happiness, success...

The list of what you potentially stand to miss out on is horrendously long. So Live in the moment. Concentrate on the here and now. Give all your energy in that moment to what you are doing now. There is a time and a place for multi-tasking, however a lot of your day needs focus to truly achieve.

90. Punctuality is a BIG thing to some people. Being on time shows you respect that persons valuable time, you respect that person and genuinely care about the outcome of the meeting. If you struggle with punctuality speed up your clock and get respecting.

91. You know when you get a bee in your bonnet about something and you think "I know I am right" and yet other times you are swayed by what other people say. What makes that happen do you think?

Do you think you truly trust in your ability to make the right decisions?

And if you get it wrong is that a big deal?

Think on it because you will love tomorrow's golden nugget...

92. Einstein said "A person that never made a mistake never tried something new" and guess what new things can lead to?

So go on make a few mistakes, learn some lessons and try something new, now where could that lead?

93. Fear grips us all, but it's your attitude to fear that will allow you to achieve success – as I like to say "Get so far out of your comfort zone you can't see it anymore." A bit scary but it works. Not for you?

Then ask yourself how do you eat a mountain of cheese?

Just one bite at a time!

Know your natural way to deal with a comfort zone & it will power you up for every fearful moment in your future.

94. Before you even walk in the office do you prioritise what is on the agenda for the day? When you left the office last night did you clearly visualise what needed to be achieved the next day?

It is imperative to productivity and your success and improves focus for your goals to achieve success.

95. If you were to consider every minute as £1 how much more carefully would you choose to spend your time?

And if you looked at where you chose to spend your time would it have been the most productive use of your time?

If you showed your accountant where you had spent your time would they agree?

Be honest with yourself – Your accountant would want tried and tested results…..so £1 a minute, how productive are you?

96. The last time you set a goal for yourself or your business, did you factor in your commitments outside of work?

You see one of the biggest reasons business women fail in their goals, is because they do not factor in that little thing called….life.

When you plan a goal ensure you have time for all areas of life and watch success head your way.

97. Smile – no really smile. No better still laugh. Did you know children laugh hundreds of times a day and us adults are lucky if we make 20. What is that doing for your health?

Your wellbeing?

Ok so life can be hard work, business can be tough, but having a laugh here and there is not illegal, it doesn't make you an unprofessional business woman, it makes you a happy one. And guess what type of people most people like to be around?

98. When there are a million possibilities to the problem in hand and you just don't know which to choose sit and write every single one down. And when you think you can't come up with another idea. Keep going. You see the first 20 or so ideas are the ones your brain has been contemplating and keeping you awake at night with. As you dig deeper your subconscious brain powers up and starts sharing its wealth of knowledge. Somewhere in the later part of your list is your answer. Coaching business women has proved that to me a ton of times!

99. Ever have a day where you feel like you are floating from one unimportant task to another when you know fore well you SHOULD be doing something else?

What is creating the road block?

Is it you just don't want to?

Have you bigged it up to a huge task, when in actual fact it will only take you a couple of hours?

Be honest with yourself, stop floating and get on with it!

100. Create the buzz around all that you do and people will be flocking to your door – well you're brilliant aren't you?

So let that brightness shine through in everything you do. Stop hiding because it's damaging your success.

101. Write a letter – in this world where everything can go at the speed of light (or is that sound?) take the time to write to someone – it speaks volumes that you care. And guess how that person will chose to remember you?

102. Get inspired – if you had an hour to yourself what would put you in the zone?

Make you feel ready for anything?

What works for you?

Knowing this will help on even the tough days, when there aren't buckets of time, but you need an instant lift that isn't caffeine or chocolate or wine shaped!

103. Do you know where you new customers came from?

Do you know where your latest big opportunity came from?

If you don't know this information how can you do more of that?

104. When you think about your life are you happy?

Really genuinely happy?

Do you not deserve that?

It's worth a moment of your time today, right? And a little note, not that happiness you get from a new pair of shoes, but that internal happiness that you will find yourself thinking of for days and smiling.

105. Who in your world makes you feel special, loved, valued?

If your world is full of people like that it can make your feel like you can get through anything.

Not got those people around you?

Time to start looking.

Got those people around you?

Would you say you are appreciating them?

106. Leaving the office in a mess because "You just gotta get outta here!" is a sense of escape in the evening but what about the next day? How are you going to feel when you walk into that mess?

Get organised – your working day will love you for it.

107. If life truly is a box of chocolates and you never know what you are going to get, how comes all boxes of chocolates come with a choccie guide?

What would be on your choccie guide?

That's a metaphor for what would be in your life, stop thinking about that chocolate and start thinking about what is on your guide to your life – it's your thought for the day.

108. Shoes – they come in all shapes and sizes but the fact is some days are just not killer heel days. Some days are comfy "I have a million things to do and need to be bursting with energy" Days.

How "bursting with energy" are you going to feel in killer heels?

Tell yourself you know you look good in anything, and give yourself the right to leave the house truly ready for it. How self-satisfied can you secretly feel when you slip your comfy shoes off at the end of the day and your feet are one part of you that still feels fresh and ready for anything!

109. Putting it off?

Is there a conversation that is a bit confrontational that you just don't want to have?

Putting it off, only makes it worst. Speak up and be proud of what you have to say.

Still not sure?

Write down everything you want to say and sit on it for a few days. How many times have you walked away from a conversation and thought "I should have said that!" This process allows you to do just that.

110. Honesty is always the best policy and people in business appreciate that honesty. It's not always the easiest course of action, but it is one that is truly admired and appreciated and showcases your professionalism. Not sure how to do this? Head to the back of this book to access my confidential mastermind group.

111. Ever thought about your work station?

How close to your computer screen do you sit? Did you know you should sit an arm's length away?

I.e. stretch your arm out and your laptop should be at the end of those fingers. If it's not your risking eye strain. That's not nice for your eyes, your concentration or the ability to keep the motivation and results going all day.

112. Chipped nail polish is not good for you or your success – don't believe me?

Ask anyone what chipped nail polish says and I bet it isn't positive. It will take an extra 60 seconds to whip that off. Chipped nails by the way says too busy, too lazy, don't care, and many other words that I just don't use. Now do you fancy hearing them in your subconscious all day?

I didn't think so.

113. Clock watching?

That's not good. Whatever you are doing you have to find a way to get enjoyment out of it. However, revolting. Even if it is just

"I can't wait to have this done and not do it again!" If you clock watch your life away – it sounds like something needs to change – now what could that be?

114. Everyone is doing their best at all the times. It's just what they think is the best thing to do won't always match up to yours. But it gets you thinking right "Everyone is doing their best." Even that car that just cut you up at the lights, and the guy that barged in the queue in front of you. Still doing their best.

115. Wow you are amazing! Right now as your reading this you're breathing, growing hair, thinking about what to have for tea, whether you answered that email, how long will it take to finish that job, did you pay the credit card and a million other things. Clever aren't you?

Just a little reminder, really though, remember all day how amazing you truly are. It will give you a real boost for the whole day!

116. The next time you walk into a networking opportunity – tell yourself I'm going to walk out of here with 4/5 business cards for some great potential leads/opportunities. Even if they don't start that way, great relationships can lead to some fantastic things – so connect – where could it take you?

And it's not just at a networking event you can grab those great opportunities. Who's that in front of you in the queue?

117. Number crunching is not much fun for many of us (thankfully Accountants do love it) however everyone needs to understand the numbers. What numbers do you need to understand in your business and in your personal finances?

Shutting your eyes to them does not make them go away. Get crunching.

118. Yesterday we talked about crunching today we are talking about munching. You put rubbish in, guess what you are going to get out?

Love that body and feed it well. I've met too many business women who have sacrificed one area of their life in the pursuit of another, bring them all in alignment and you will achieve more so love the body you are in.

119. Did you know different colours create different thoughts in our head?

Did you know that the colour red makes us think that that person is more likely to be competitive, faster and more athletic but possibly have a lower IQ?

What are your colours saying about you?

How are colours impacting on you in your work place?

120. Studies have shown goals that are written down are more likely to be achieved.

Where are yours written down?

At a bottom of a pile of paperwork on your desk?

Filed away?

Or subtly in your subconscious line of sight all the time?

Allow your subconscious to really power up on your goals.

121. When it comes to your business do you collect testimonials like a bee collecting pollen? Because you should, but don't just collect them, use them and Tell the WORLD!

This is not bragging big headedness this is raising awareness to those around you of all you can achieve and help them with. Be in their minds for all the right reasons.

122. If you had a jar of motivation what would be in there?

Knowing that on a good day can power up a tough one. That pair of heels you adore?

That song?

That dress?

An extra long bath full of aromatherapy?

A photo of a special day?

A swim?

A walk?

A chat with your best mate?

What would be in your jar?

123. When was the last time you checked your Junk email – okay so most of it is junk, but sometimes a good email slips in – and it's not good to miss your emails.

Who could you be missing out on?

124. How are those 2 lists looking?

Your "Got to get done" and your "Would love to do" lists?

Still sticking with them?

Taking action?

Doesn't it feel great knowing you can achieve anything you put your mind, body and soul into?

Not happening?

What aren't you dealing with?

125. Social media is just that social, so talk to people, ask questions, share comments, ideas, stories, YouTube clips. Be a giver

not a taker. And keep your profiles up to date. You never know whose going to pop by.

126. If you don't know something, ask. If you don't you are agreeing to have that knowledge out of your reach.

How rubbish does that feel? There is always someone you can ask, that you can trust – and trust me you can include me in that list of people to trust.

127. If I told you to go get 3 new clients by the end of the month you would do things differently right?

What about if I told you to go and get 30 clients by the end of the month?

What about if I told you your hair will fall out and you will gain 20 pounds if you didn't?

Wow, funny how we can get motivated right? How powerful a motivation have you got going on right now?

128. The sun makes us feel gooood. A fresh Danish makes us feel naughty (but indulged), a compliment can make us smile, a song can make us feel light and happy. Funny how you can feel things by getting and doing things. I wonder if it could work for you the other way around – just a thought....

129. Having a tough day?

Pick up the phone, write an email, and talk to your inspirational friend, business friend, mum, sister – you are a successful business woman, not a robot – emotions and feelings are allowed. And tough days happen. Don't go it alone if you don't fancy it. People genuinely care.

130. Success needs your passion, your determination and a billion other things, although the most important 2 things it needs

are yourself belief and action!

Success is not going to knock on your door, you have got to go and knock on Successes door. And always having self belief and taking proactive action could ensure it happens.

131. Thoughts can buzz around your head sometimes for days. Disturbing your sleep and taking up too much of your brain power – get it out.

Talk about it, write your thoughts down and deal with them. It may not be much fun, but then how much fun is it forgetting important things and lacking in sleep because that thoughts been allowed to buzz around in there?

132. Marketing should have very few !! or?? And NO CAPTIAL LETTERS or changing the colour after every other word or bold type shouting it out. Why?

Because a) it is unlikely to reach your targets in box and b) how unnatural does that look?

Is that how you would talk to that person if they were in the room with you?

133. Does anyone in your world feel neglected? Have you spent too much time in the office and not enough time with your dog/ husband/friend/daughter/mum?

Or is it the other way around and the business is getting the short straw – balance can be tricky but it's essential. Are you feeling balanced today?

What could help you restore balance?

134. LinkedIn is a little beauty for effective networking, building your reputation, and showcasing your skills and successes (to enable more to come your way.)

Ideal for when you can't get out there in person. But are you using it right?

Be patient, give it a little bit of your time, join some relevant groups, check out who you should connect with, show case your successes, include your skills and get social – your success could love it!

135. Thank you is the last thought you need to have before you go to sleep. Being grateful for all you have achieved, everyone that was in your day, for all that happened, and everything else is essential to power up the next day. And if before you even open your eyes the following day and think about all the things you are grateful for, what could that do for your mindset for the day?

This is a simple exercise but very powerful if you become dedicated to it.

136. How many blogs, newsletters and emails have you signed up to that you don't read?

For one week read every single one (okay speed read) and think if I had time would I read this?

Half the time it's not even relevant to you, so unsubscribe. Although if it's useful, it can only be useful if you read it and action it. So take action today. If it overwhelms you, create a folder so it all lands straight in the folder and doesn't stop you from seeing the important "must action" emails.

137. Thank you........it's a lovely word wouldn't you say?

Who would benefit from a thank you from you?

It can be done with flowers, a phone call, a coffee, an email, a letter, a card. Even a 140 characters on Twitter can do it and it means so much. And the bonus is you get to feel good for doing it too.

138. Rubbish day?

Smile, it says "I can get through this."

Feeling blue?

Smile, it sets off them endorphins. Smiling really is powerful stuff, both on you and the people that see that gorgeous smile of yours. It sends out positive vibes as well as sending them straight back to you. Just be open minded and try it.

Go on.....

139. Have you got good news?

Don't hide it, tell the world.

It's not bragging its appreciating why you are so brilliant. But I already knew that about you! Get in touch with your local media. They love a good news story, a girl does good story. Do it right and soon you will be their "expert of choice". Now how could that feel?

140. If you had 5 minutes to change your world with as many wishes as you could cram in, what would you wish for?

Does life look remotely like that?

What one thing could you do to get you that bit closer?

Would you get in your car and drive somewhere you've never been without a Satnav, Directions or Map?

The same goes for your goals!

141. Social media- is it a distraction or a useful tool in your business day?

If you can't answer that question, it's highly likely it comes under the first category.

Testing and measuring your marketing is key – even on social media. And remember even if you don't use it for business, it's still a tool others may use to check you out. What would they find on your page?

Is that the image you want the professional world to have of you?

142. You look at some business women and think "Wow, why can't I be like that?"

The fact is you can be and you possibly already are. And guess what, it's highly likely they are thinking "Why can't I be like that?"

Funny old world, right?

Could it be time for a new thought?

Change your perspective and you can change your actions and results.

143. Do you have days were you work tirelessly for hours and hours and hours without a break, "Wow you think. I'm so good."

Guess what?

You would be even more productive had you had a short break here and there. Google's staff does that all the time!

144. Have you ever entered any awards or competitions for your business?

Why not?

You're brilliant so go tell the world and get some recognition for what you do.

It's all good for your reputation, media and PR opportunities (and success!)

145. Do you feel like the most productive, successful, happiest business woman in the world?

Well you should, because you are what you think you are... ooooo scary!

146. 1, 2, 3, 4 numbers can be useful right? Do you love your lists? Prioritise what needs to be done today and feel like a productive super star when you leave work today.

147. If you left the house without your normal make up, hair style, outfit would the world be different?

Would you get treated differently?

Would you be less successful?

Do clothes maketh the woman or does the woman maketh the woman?

148. Always do the worst job first. It creates momentum for the day. Leaving it to the end of the day sucks the life out of your productive energy for the next day.

149. If at first you don't succeed give up – no I didn't think that was right either, but if it isn't working what do you need to do differently?

150. If today was your last day on this planet, would you say you had truly done all you could to get what you want in life?

Were there a few excuses?

A few regrets?

It's not your last day (Phew!) so forget about regrets and excuses and go get that life!

151. Do your customers make you happy?

If not do you have the right customers?

Are you attracting the right type of customers? Great customers pay on time, respect your space, and give you time to deliver amazingly, do yours?

By the way great bosses and work colleagues do the same.

152. Mirroring another person's body language can be a great way of subconsciously connecting with that person. But don't make it look obvious, that is just pure annoying and will lose you their trust pretty quickly.

153. Email can be a lifeline, a gem in your business, an essential nugget to success. BUT it can also be a big fat waste of your valuable time.

Do you have something important to get on with?

Turn that email notification sound off, switch email off and get on.

Love email that much?

Reward yourself at the end of the working hour with 5 emails. Now get on!

154. Public speaking is a great way to promote you and your business.

Scared of it?

Then step up to the stand and go for it anyway, the more you do it the easier it gets (trust me I've seen this happen to so many business women – the more you do it, the easier and the more natural it will feel) and if you love public speaking, what could you say different today?

Don't risk your message going stale and people turning off. If you really struggle at the back of this book are some resources that could make you a very powerful public speaker.

155. Don't bad mouth people. In the words of Thumper from

Bambi "If you can't say nothing nice then don't say nothing at all" If you are asked for your opinion on someone and it would only be bad things you say, say nothing. That speaks volumes just as well.

156. Take one minute out to breathe deeply 3 times. Shut your eyes. And let the air flow through you. Ensure your breath is coming from the bottom of your lungs. You know that is happening if your stomach is moving and not your chest. It can be enough to focus the mind, calm you down or relieve the stress and it only takes a minute – be nice to your body – it's the only one you've got!

157. Treat advice like water into a sponge – wring out what you don't want. Short and sweet, but it works a treat!

158. Scared of public speaking?

Speak to 100 people with a microphone.

Hate picking up the phone?

Set a goal to make 5 phone calls every day.

You get the idea. Comfort zones can wreak havoc with your success. And here's the good news, after that first big one – that comfort zone will be "What comfort zone?" Because the more action you take the smaller and smaller that fear gets, until it's gone. And if that doesn't work you could fit into the people that hate big goals, so to get out of your comfort zone take one small action.

Scared of public speaking?

Agree to a 60 seconds elevator pitch.

Hate picking up the phone?
Make one call every day.

You can use this on all fears big and brave or small and spirited.

Cool right?

159. Got a job you don't want to do?

Post on your social media you are going to do it. Let your online world motivate you. (Or shame you into doing it!)

160. Music can soothe, excite, motivate, inspire and even release endorphins which can increase your pain threshold, make you feel happier and healthier – what music does what to you?

161. Is there a job that you look at and say "mmm that's big, I'll do that when I have the time to dedicate to that."

Guess what?

It's like a stain on your favourite top. Your eyes are drawn to it constantly – so deal with it today, and get it done.

162. When was the last time you had a day off? If you don't step back once in a while you won't see the wood for the trees. Go get yourself your Eureka moments – they could be hiding in that space.

163. Don't keep putting things off, if someone set a deadline, they set that for a reason. (Even if you don't get what that reason is!)

How miffed are they going to be when the deadline passes and you didn't deliver?

What does that do for your business relationship?

If you can't deliver pick up the phone and be honest.

164. Credibility takes a life time to get and can take a minute to be lost – build, grow and protect yours.

165. Picking up the phone can lead to the meetings you need to get the customers you want, the opportunities you crave and the

success you deserve.

So what are you waiting for?

Don't send another email, pick up the phone.

166. Rebranding every five minutes will not change what you deliver or what people think of you. Concentrate on building a great reputation and great relationships with the right people.

167. If you are scared of doing something, do it anyway. Who wants a fear in their business right? The quickest way to squash it is to face it head on – but go prepared. What would prepare you? Do you need new skills? A new mind set? A new belief? And if that doesn't work, how does it feel allowing an obstacle to your success to stick around?

168. Sending emails at 3 o'clock in the morning may help you clear the load mentally and physically but what does it say about you? If you really HAVE to do it, then schedule their delivery time for sensible o'clock.

169. There is no shame in saying this is not working. If something is not working for you admitting it is the first step to fixing it. So don't berate yourself, praise yourself for getting started on what will work.

170. Do you have a business / success / career / goals / life plan?

Is it stuffed in a file somewhere or is it like a much loved teddy?

A bit threadbare, every inch known, loved and well used?

If it's not how are you going to achieve what you set for your business / success / career / goals / life this year?

171. Helping a local charity is good for the charity and good for

business too. It can help you get free publicity, get noticed and a warm fuzzy feeling inside – everyone's a winner!

172. Have you created residual income in your business?

How could you do that?

How could you be off doing one thing and being paid for something else, somewhere else?

If you don't know, who could help you come up with some answers?

173. If you say you are going to do something however minor or major – do it!

What does it say about you if you don't?

What messages are you sending yourself for future goals/aspirations or tough chores?

More importantly what does it say about your business and success?

174. Body language can be what you pick up on long before your head is giving you what you want to hear. Ask yourself what subtleties in a person's body language are being given away? Opening your mind to these subtleties can power up your relationships and help you get more of what you want.

175. A tidy desk creates a tidy mind. An organised desk creates an organised mind, and an empty desk creates an empty mind – what does your desk say about you?

176. Competitors are not always competitors – sometimes they are opportunities to learn, to share, to help, to cross promote and to grow your business – are you seeing your competitors differently now?

177. Did you know there is literally billions of billions of content whizzing around online every day. Would you say yours stands out for all the right reasons? Go on, go Google yourself....

178. What in your business life could you structure?

Could you have standard letters that you personalise?

Emails that filter away to different folders? Little things like that can make the world of difference to your busy day.

179. When was the last time you checked out your lists that we created at the beginning of this book?

A goal regularly revisited is more likely to be achieved. I'm just saying....

180. Got a huge job on your hands?

Drowning under it?

Break it into bite size chunks, think what a bite size chunk would look like and only tackle that. Don't look at the mountain, look at the steps you need to tackle to the next big rock. Remember "How do you eat a mountain of Cheese?" that's right, "One bite at a time!"

181. Surveys are a great way of finding out what your customers think, so you don't have to guess. And Survey monkey lets you do that for free. Cool right?

182. Social media is a free marketing tool. But only if you have a strategy and test and measure your results. Otherwise it's a tool of procrastination costing you one of your most valuable assets – Your Time!

183. If you can't explain it simply then you don't understand it. Einstein was so right and it's true in business too. Do you keep it simple?

184. You have to be clear about what you want otherwise how are you going to get it?

Got that?

Do you feel that you are really translucent on what you want?

185. Shake it up a bit today, do things out of routine, phone instead of email, surprise people, do things differently and see what happens. It can work wonders on your motivation and creativity. Not sure you can get to grips with this?

Start by getting dressed and ready for the day in a slightly different way. It will help your brain process what you are aiming to do and help you shake it up. Doing things slightly differently can have a major impact on your success levels in all that you do.

186. Your email signature is another opportunity to promote your business, your skills and talents, and to connect with people. Does it include your telephone number, website, social media links?

Do you make it easy for people to connect and interact with you?

Got one of your favourite testimonials in there?

Remember to keep it short and sweet.

187. Your first post to a new follower should not be "Hi take a look at our website"

Would you do that if you met that person in real life?

Then don't do it on social media either.

188. When networking if you don't understand what someone

does, ask. If you don't, how are you going to be a great networker and connect them to the right people and the right opportunities?

It's essential.

189. Does your marketing have a call to action? If not how will people be reminded of what you want them to do?

For that matter does your phone technique or email have a call to action too?

190. When was the last time you congratulated yourself on being an amazing business woman?

Well I know you are, so tell yourself how gorgeously brilliant you are!

Get specific as you drive to work, queue at the bank or make a cuppa and list examples of your brilliance. It will be our little secret, but will help you feel great all day. What could that do for your success today?

191. If you feel like quitting or giving up. Ask yourself the reason why?

Is it a justified reason?

Are you hiding behind fear?

Do you need to learn new skills, hold on to a new belief and get rid of an old unhelpful one?

192. Little things go a long way. A smile, a please, a thank you, a hello, a deep breath, a glass of water, a cup of tea.

Which would work for you right now?

Don't neglect yourself in pursuit of success. In the long run it won't work.

193. As you walk anywhere today say this in your head to the beat of your feet "I am a successful business woman, who achieves whatever I set my mind to" No one need know you are saying it right?

A bit like those bottom clenches we are all supposed to do at the checkout queue right?

194. Phones are there for a reason. We do not hang on to our phones 24 hours a day for no reason, pick it up!

Make someone's day and connect the old fashion way. It speaks volumes about you as a business woman, as a person, as a friend.

195. Success is in the mind's eye – so what does success look like to you?

How close are you?

What have you already achieved?

What is coming next?

If you don't ask these questions how can you be heading for great things?

196. When you look in the mirror what do you see?

I see a very talented successful business woman reading this.

Not seeing it?

Look harder, you will....

197. Too hot, too cold, too bulky clothes, uncomfortable chair? It will all affect your performance and your concentration. Get comfortable and power up your results. Funny how we don't notice our clothes until someone says something right? That mind of yours is very clever.

198. Marketing is like exercise – to benefit you have to do it regularly. Not liking that idea? Find a way so that you do.

199. Exercise comes in many forms, but however you chose to do it, do it regularly to power up your success. A healthy body is a happy body.

200. Is there a piece of technology letting you down?

How much wasted time each day do you have to put up with before you get it fixed?

Think about all that time you have wasted over the past week, month, year?

Is THAT a thought that makes you squirm and cringe and enough to get you to fix it?

Think about all the cool stuff you could have done with that time.

THAT should do it.

201. Who knows Ron?

Well Ron steals your time, your energy, your productivity, your motivation. So make sure you know Ron and stay well clear. Can't find your Ron?

Well what about if I called him "Later Ron?" mmmmm thought you would find him, now get rid of him!

The power is in the NOW.

Do It Now!

202. When things get tough, who can you rely on?

Who can you guarantee will cheer you up, motivate and inspire you?

Knowing this is essential to get you through tough times with a smile.

203. If I could give you one piece of advice that would stick with you for life it would be this..... Believe in you, like I believe in you as you read this right now.

Powerful stuff right?

Now go out there and be amazing!

204. Some days feel like they are there to really rack you off, to make you explode, to feel very gggggggrrrrr (Thats the technical term for it!) Days like that you need to step away. Give yourself a break. A 20% break from your normal working day has been proven to increase productivity and creativity. And it's good for the soul too.

205. You don't have to be an expert at everything. Are you dealing with something really really tough?

That you hate?

That you just can't get your head around? Learn about it and if all else fails outsource.

206. When was the last time you picked up the phone and had a chat with your customers?

Do your customers feel loved?

Only one way to find out and that is to ask them.

Do your suppliers feel like you care about them?

What could that do to the service you receive?

What could it do to Your Success?

207. When was the last time you did a selfless act?

Giving leads to people you know. Promoted someone without being asked to. Written a review and asking for nothing in return. The science that a selfless act is good for you as much as it is good for the other person.

208. The next time you are networking and meeting new people, take a moment to look at that new contacts business card, comment on it, on what they do, etc. Make them feel special. It took ages for them to create that, get the design just right. Show you care and start that relationship in a great way. Even if they didn't personally design that card it symbolises what they do with their day all day every day. Show it matters to you too.

209. If you are sending emails with too many !!! or bold type or BIG LETTERS or tons of different colours they are likely to be classed as too "salesly" and who wants to be sold at right?

(By the way, often they also fail software designed to keep that spam out of your targets inbox anyway.)

210. Commenting on other people's blogs is a great way to interact, share your views, get known as an expert in your field and raise awareness of that person's blog. (Which makes you a very nice person) and is great for your online marketing strategy.

211. Someone did a great job for you?

Tell the world on their LinkedIn page, Facebook profile, Twitter account, Google review, etc. Send them a testimonial and tell them they can use it anywhere they like on their marketing. Thank yous are so valuable in business and help lead people to their next customers. Are you using your testimonials productively?

212. Did you know it takes someone about 3 seconds to decide if the website they are looking at is any good?

So what are you doing to ensure they stick around on yours?

213. When you leave work tonight as you drive/walk/cycle/ swim/canoe home think about what went well. What could have gone better?

What you are going to start with tomorrow? What must be completed by the end of the week?

What you are working on to get you nearer to your year's goals?

And then allow your mind to wander and drift into home mode. Think about what's for dinner?

Who will greet you when you get there?

What you are going to wear?

What needs to be done in the home?

What you are going to do to relax tonight? Allow your mind to catch up to your body and move from work mode to home mode effortlessly. And in the morning reverse it!

214. Did you know the human brain sends more messages a day than all the business women in the US and UK put together?

Well that might not be true, but it's a lot!

Allow your mind the space to work through those thoughts. TIP that won't happen if every minute of every day is full of stuff. Clear 10 minutes a day for time to let that brain do its wowness.

215. Waiting for an important phone call, email, letter?

It's a big opportunity and you can't get it out of your mind?

Then you are agreeing to give the power of your day over to someone else. Oooooo that sounds bad right?

Box it up, get busy, dance, sing, work, play, read, write, text, walk, talk but keep that mind full of good stuff – it won't happen any faster but you will be a lot happier waiting.

216. Type on colour is harder to read. It may look pretty, but people want to read things quickly and get on and that can't happen if they are struggling to read something. Go on, make life easier for others – they will love you for it!

217. You are an expert, a leader, a teacher. Everyone is. You just have to find what it is you are an expert at so that you can lead the way, teach and share. It's great for you, your business and your success.

218. Done a great job?

Tell the world. If you are not proud of what you have achieved and don't think you are great, why will anyone else?

It doesn't need to be arrogant does it?

219. Not sure what people think of your services and products ask someone what they really think. And not your Nan/Hubby/Sister/Mum or best friend, who would say everything you do is great. Someone who will be critical in a nice way and allow you to offer an even better service.

220. Action, Action and more Action will get you where you want to go. Visualisation is great but without Action, it's just a day dream. Daydreams are nice but not as good for success as visualisation and action. So Action is the order of the day.

221. Sometimes admitting you made a mistake is tough, but it still has to be done. How can you fix something if you are not prepared to admit you even did it wrong?

222. Need a bit of inspiration?

Don't we all, because some days just don't run like a speedy Gonzalez. Days like that, what should you do?

Give up?

No, I didn't think so either. Pick up the phone and ask someone, Tweet it, share it and get the boost you need.

223. Networking is like anything else in your business it needs a level of commitment from you, the right actions and regular input – If you fall off of people's radar guess what, I bet your competitors aren't. It gets you thinking right?

224. Drink water, no really drink water. A dehydrated brain is an unhappy brain. Actually it's also less efficient, less creative, less motivated, less focussed and a lot of other things a busy business woman like you could do without having to deal with. And who wants one of those?

So drink water.

225. Bad suppliers are a waste of your precious time. It may take time to change but think how much time, effort and money you could save in the long run. That should give you incentive enough, knowing that your long term success will get a boost from your action today.

226. A smiling face on your desk is a great thing to look at every day. It reminds you how much you are loved, it tells you people care, and it brings back great memories. What a great emotion to create from the comfort of your work place every day. (No matter who you have to talk to on the phone a photo can be sharing a thousand happy thoughts in the background at the same time!

227. "Sticks and Stones may break my bones but words will never hurt me." Actually this is not true. Stand in front of a mirror and say really mean things to yourself. Now stand in front of the mir-

ror and say great things about yourself. Hint – I've done this in a roomful of business woman and been able to prove that negative words can directly impact on our physical being too and make you weaker. So what words are you going to hear today?

228. Your gut instinct can be very powerful. Trust it. Quite often you will be picking up subconsciously what you need to know long before your conscious brain gets the idea.

229. A problem shared is a problem halved. Well it is if you share it with the right person. Know today who would be the right person (people) to lean on.

230. Those lists should be getting tons of ticks by now. Do you tick off what you have achieved? Put a line through it or is there a severe lack of progress going on?

It's only you and your life you are letting down, and I would hate to see that happen, after all you only deserve the best.

231. Email marketing is a great way to keep in touch, keep on people's radar and share your good news, ideas and solutions. But don't overdo it, keep it regular and gauge your reader's interest levels. Remember your clients are just as mega busy as you are.

232. No one on their death bed says "I wish I had washed the kitchen floor more often" just saying.

233. Sometimes you look in the mirror and you say horrible things about yourself. How unkind is that?

Would you do that to your best mate?

Your mum?

About time you gave yourself the same level of kindness don't you think?

234. You are one step closer to success by the time you finish reading this sentence. Wow that would be great wouldn't' it?

What could actually get you that step closer to your heart's desire?

Allow that question to wander around the recesses of your mind all day.

235. Twitter, Twatter, fact is many business women have Twitter accounts they rarely use. Hoping that by design it will create more customers, more recognition and more success. Guess what?

You have got to be in it to win it, get it?

What social media accounts have you set up and ignored?

If someone stumbles upon them what would they think?

236. Are you one of those people that hands out tons of great ideas and advice?

Do you take your advice, and do as you say?

Guess what, if you don't, your credibility could take a nose dive.

237. Tiredness kills. Tiredness also deadens the brain, leads to mistakes and grumpiness. Now who wants those?

Being tired is not a crime. Give in and take a break. Rest, love yourself. Go on, you are allowed.

Are you reading this thinking "You don't understand, I've got so much to do!" If you've got that much to do, do you really want to be doing it twice putting things right or spending twice the amount of time on things because you can't think straight?

238. You can't dictate when someone buys from you, but you can have a say in who they choose to use. Keep on people's radar and

make sure it's you they choose!

239. Comfort zones can get smaller and smaller if you don't challenge them. Go on, you can do it. Step so far out of your comfort zone you can't see it anymore. It works wonders for success.

240. When was the last time you backed up your documents, your files, your pictures? Did you check it worked?

It is a really boooorrrrinnnngggg subject but crucial to every business woman. Ask any IT expert and they will tell you the same. And good practices in one area of life tend to migrate to other areas of your life too.

241.When you get to deliver your 60 seconds elevator pitch at a networking event, smile, go slowly (chances are however slowly you speak it is still too fast) don't try to cover too much, finish with your company name and your name and be less than 60 seconds – did you give them a call to action, a hook, a reason to come and talk to you to find out more?

Because THAT'S what it's all about.

242. Bad spelling and punctuation can really annoy some people. Even if it does not bother you it will work against you if you are looking to connect with that person. The idea is to work to their likes and passions, not yours.

243. When you started work this morning, did you have a clear outline of the tasks to tackle today?

It's essential you do this to ensure the money making work is scheduled along with the day to day stuff. (And it creates momentum to keep going – which makes you feel good!)

244. Just because with business to business you are allowed

to utilise that businesses contact details, automatically adding them to your mailing list is not the nicest way to start a beautiful successful relationship and is less likely to lead to your marketing getting read. Build a relationship, build a customer.

245. Putting off a horrible job does not make it go away, it just makes it bigger and uglier and more scary and your mind will constantly berate you for not getting it done. Now who wants that?

Do you fancy that?

Best get it done then.

246. Create the Buzz – creating a buzz around everything about you and your business is infectious stuff. How can you get buzzy?

247. Don't fight the person you are, work with it. Don't know who you really are? Time to explore that right?

248. Don't be ashamed of what your version of success looks like. Everyone's ideal of success looks different and everyone wants different things. That's the great thing about this thing called life. But craving what you think you should want is fatal for happiness and success.

249. Just thought I would remind you how brilliant you are. You hadn't forgotten had you?

250. Some days just feel like days from hell don't they?

The cat pukes up on your best shoes, the car won't start, your broadband goes down, you're put on hold for the umpteenth time only to explain the same thing again and again and then it chucks it down with rain and you have a big meeting to attend looking like a proverbial drown rat. The only option at times like that is to smile, laugh and just accept that, that's life. It won't fix your day, but it will get you through it a lot easier. The alternative is to let it get you down and impact on every last minute until you shut your eyes that night in your bed, is that a better choice?

251. Self development is a dish best served regularly – a bit like that glass of water that I mentioned to you – and by the way, it can just be a positive word in your own ear, it doesn't have to be a year trekking Tibet "finding yourself."

252. Sometimes walking away is the best option, and other times sticking it out is key. I bet you REALLY know which is which right?

Okay, but sometimes it's not so easy to do what needs to be done right?

I know what that's like too. Trust in yourself and you will work it out.

253. Sleep, food, fresh air, and water are key to your body's health. Just in case you forget, you are not a robot, and you do need all of the above. By the way you also need love, kindness, peace and quiet and space to think. And the occasional hug and friendly coffee is pretty useful too! The successful business woman forgets these things at her peril.

254. Remember I told you not to sweat the small stuff?

Are you?

Remember what a mess it makes of your outfit and your life, now do you want that?

255. What makes you feel successful?

Is it an outfit, a look at your bank statement, a memory of your biggest client?

Whatever it is, remind yourself of it regularly. It's a handy way to keep heading in the right direction. Boosting your motivation and determination to keep aiming for your goals.

256. Negativity is something that can seep into any life. Watch out for it and banish it. It can all start from one little thought, but it can have a major impact on your day.

257. Remember yesterday I told you it all starts with a thought. It's not just the bad stuff that starts with a thought you know. A great mindset also starts with a thought, a belief. In fact the most amazing inventions, business women and successes all started with a thought – Wow, powerful stuff. What thought are you programming into your mind today?

258. If you don't interact with the people you want to work with how are you going to start to work for them?

259. Do you know what your ideal client looks like?

If you don't, the next time you are networking or talking on a one to one basis, how can people be on the lookout for your ideal client for you?

Share your ideal client ideas with people you get to know and they too will have that idea on their radar too. Half the work, twice the chance of success.

260. Never, ever, ever, ever give up. Winston Churchill had the right idea.

261. A pen to hand when networking is very handy, not just for you. It means if you say something incredibly useful and interesting and let's be honest you will, the other person can write it down on your card – that should get them remembering you for

all the right reasons. By the way making notes shows others you are serious about helping them and being useful to them in the future. All good for your reputation.

262. Before you even arrive at that meeting, networking meeting, or event – have you thought what your ideal outcome would be? Makes it harder to achieve if you have not given it any thought, right?

263. Got a burning ambition?

Is it hidden in your mind, or are you planning to achieve it?

Life is not something that will wait around for you. Today is the day to get on with those burning ambitions of yours. Positively think about achieving them and you will.

264. You can't possibly know the answer to everything, but there is always someone that will know the answers you need. Who are the people you can rely on?

Where can you get the information you need, to get the answers that will power up your success?

265. Imagine its 10 to 5 in the afternoon and you are heading out of the office within the hour, to enjoy your evening. What are you leaving on your desk for the following morning?

Is that likely to motivate you or drag you down in the morning – why not set yourself up for success. Clear the dregs, Plan the next day's priorities, you get the idea...

266. Some things in life are never going to feel easy right?

So you have 2 choices. 1, Put up and moan and berate every time you have to do them or 2, learn some new skills. Oh you could outsource it right? (mmm that's 3 choices – well I do like to over deliver!)

267. When you get through to the person you want to speak with on the phone, it's always nice to say "Do you have time to speak now or should I call back later" for 2 reasons. Firstly it says "Hey I respect your time" and 2 "If you don't speak to me now, I will be calling back, so let's get this sorted now shall we." Tomorrow I will share another useful phone titbit

268. On the phone never say "Is now a good time to talk, or are you busy" Why? Because how many business women do you know that are not busy? You just gave them the perfect excuse to put the phone down.

269. Social media is just that social. But did you know that while more women than men are on social media, more men use it for business successfully?

It's free, it's powerful and if you do it right it works for your business success. How can you power up your success rate?

270. If in doubt leave it out. Well you know me and nuggets to easily remember, if it does not feel right, there is no need to say no, just "Let me get back to you" "Let me sleep on that" however you chose to do it, if your gut is shouting at you to stop, cease, desist, no, then listen.

271. It's never too late to learn a new skill. But be realistic, go at your pace, learn in a way that suits you and set goals that honour you, not a business woman that you might know. It's a sure fire way to success if you honour your style of learning.

272. Crank up the music, sing, dance, and smile. Why?

Why not?

273. If you are committed to growth and development of your business, how exactly will you get more customers and make more money?

Have you a written plan of action?

A clear outline of what you will do and by when?

Have you a succinct sentence that explains simply what your goal is?

274. If you could shave 5 minutes off of your wasted hours in the day. And let's be honest we all have a few seconds here and there that are not utilised. What impact could that have over a week?

Instead of counting calories (and we all know how much fun that is!) counting up your minutes could gain you precious time in your week – now what could that do for success?

275. How could you sell more of what you do to the same people?

It's probably going to start by interacting with them, so what would be next?

How do your current customers like to hear from you?

What do they like to know?

What do they want?

What do they need?

Know the answers to these questions and utilise them to sell more to your current customers.

276. Who wants free publicity for their business? Get generous and work with a charity. One that matters to you or is local and make sure you tell the world. That means including local press, right?

Charities and local charitable organisations don't just want funds, they also want to raise their profile and working with local businesses is a great way for them to get in front of important business to business clients, now how popular does that make you?

277. "Fake it until you make it" is not always the coolest answer, but "believe you can be that what you wish to be" is ultra cool. Then you've got to do the work to ensure you get there, but it all starts with that vision and trust. So what do you need to believe?

278. Having a good team of people around you ensures continued success for you. Who is in your mastermind group for success?

279. So many business women go out looking for new customers, but have you utilised the ones you already have?

Sell more, more often.

Something new and complimentary, offer them a special offer that new customers can't access – go on, make your customers feel loved. It's far more likely to create a sense of loyalty if they feel genuinely appreciated and that good value, excellent service and great innovative products are automatically heading their way.

280. If you are working from home sometimes. Whether you are working for a global giant or are self employed you need to be seen. Get visual, get noticed. Power up your success.

281. Ever noticed how very confident people don't fail?

Wrong.

They do fail; they just don't take it as the final answer.

282. Competitors are not always a bad thing. Know yours. Who is a direct competition?

What is your unique offering compared to them?

And sometimes working WITH competitors can lead to bigger contracts, shared ideas and new opportunities. Creative thinking when it comes to your competitors can be good for business.

283. Can you easily and simply describe what you do?

This is a key skill for every business woman. Practice today as you drive to work, or stand in that queue or wait at that meeting.

284. Inspiration does not always come to you by staring at the screen for longer. Walk away, walk the dog, walk the phone – a 20 minute break can be enough to stir the inspirational juices. Not just a crazy idea, there is a lot of science and research (and happy clients who will tell you this is true. Don't be a martyr to the task, it rarely works.)

285. A good business book, can be packed with ideas that you can put into action in your business and your life. A bad one can leave you feeling dejected and useless, and waste your precious time. Choose wisely.

286. Insurance is an essential thing in every business. Are you insured?

Its money you could so put to a better use right?

Say that to someone who got an investigation or whose offices burnt down or been burgled.....

287. If you don't see a business woman you know for a long time, what do you do?

Just dismiss it?

What about an email, a "How are you, and what's going on in your life/business?" or picking up the phone. Showing you care stands you apart from your competition, and that gets you remembered for all the right reasons.

288. When you get someone's business card, what do you do with it?

Do you email them soon after and thank them for their time?

Track them down on social media?

Store their information in your online data base with notes to remind you how, where and when you met them and how you could be useful to them and vice a versa?

That would take precious time right?

So why did you bother taking their card if you weren't going to utilise the information on it?

And remember for most things now there's an app, find the right app and you get the right information stored in the right way so you can use it in the right ways too.

289. That business card I wanted you to get maximum benefit out of yesterday. Did you email that person within 48 hours?

If not, guess who is slipping off their radar?

Ensure that if you network you have time after the event to follow up effectively. Or you just wasted your time and your money, scary right?

290. Checking out a new contacts website, is the height of sincerity and shows you really do want to understand that business, so that you can be a great networker. Also the next time you meet them, you have an automatic starting point for conversation. And who in business doesn't want to be encouraged to talk more about their business and what it can do for you?

Go on, power up your networking.

291. Enthusiasm is contagious. Is there a spark of enthusiasm in your business?

In your life?

In you?

Heck let's get enthusiastic here, is there an all mighty explosive plethora of oozing enthusiasm in all that you do?

People will love to get involved if there is.

292. There are so many hours in the day, are you getting maximum benefit out of them?

What needs to change?

Have you created poor habits?

Take a look and be honest with yourself. It can really power up the use of your time, your productivity and ultimately your results.

293. Putting off horrible jobs makes them no easier, only bigger and uglier in your head. Make today the day where you say. "Ggrr-rrr your gone, your outta here, your dust/toast/history" in a 70's western style voice. Or just get on with it.....your choice!

294. Today shake things up, Have tea instead of coffee, deal with your post before your emails/phone messages. Ring someone first thing instead of later. A little change can make a big difference to the impact on your day. So let's power your day up!

295. Being in tune with your body can lead to optimum health. I wonder what being in tune with your customers could do.

296. Are you learning something new?

Practice is very important, and then so is practice, oh and don't forget to practice. You see the more you practice pretty soon, it will be 2nd nature. Think driving a car/riding a bike...

297. Did someone do a great job for you?

Tell them. You would want people to do the same for you wouldn't you?

298. The person that walks in the room moaning and groaning will find they have plenty of space to think (and it's probably unhelpful thoughts). The person that walks into a room smiling and open eared is always the one that never runs out of friends and new contacts for their business success or lacks good thoughts in their head too.

Just a thought.

299. Listening is a skill that can take years to master. If you struggle. Say in your head every word the other person says and you will find you create the space for them to talk and feel really appreciated. If you really struggle, count to 10 before you speak.

300. The toughest of times have to be got through somehow and when you just don't know how you are going to manage, only concentrate on putting one foot in front of the other. We all have a limit, so if you feel like you have reached yours visualising the final goal, the big aim might just be a crippling step too far. So just concentrate on getting one foot in front of the other. Step, step, step...

301. If you work in an isolating environment what can that do for your business success? One thing is for sure that negative voice of yours will do its best to be heard. What can you do to shut it up?

302. Everyone has to deal with rejection. But guess what?

Rejection is one step closer to acceptance, to that contract, that new customer. Unless of course you give up, then it will always be just as far away....

303. Smile and the world smiles with you. Frown and your about as much fun as a hurricane at a barbeque. But where can you go where you can be yourself and get the support and comfort you need to succeed?

Sometimes you need someone you can have a really good moan and groan to, but chose wisely.

304. Getting your customers from word of mouth is great right?

But what if you are looking to grow your business, move in a new direction or create a new opportunity?

It will never be enough – what else are you doing to ensure tons of happy customers always and a business growing and developing?

305. Public speaking is a great opportunity, so seize it every time. However scary it may feel. Remember I've resources to help you feel confident in any speaking engagement – from asking your boss for a pay rise, getting your dream contract or standing up for what you believe in.

306. Assume.

It's a word too many business women use, and it blocks out your success.

Why?

Assume - it makes an ASS out of U and ME (you knew that right?)

Don't assume someone got your proposal, message or email. Pick up the phone and find out. Remember everyone is busy. Knowing can lead to action. Either you get the result you want or you find out why you weren't right for them. And that can still lead to positive action.

And if you really want to put assume in it's place, what are you assuming about your capabilities? Your earning potential? It get's you thinking right? I've never seen a client that couldn't think bigger and override an assumption to achieve more.

307. Would you say you are the kind of person that looks out for opportunities?

Do you see them when they are even in front of your nose?

Knowing what a great opportunities looks like and what could be a waste of your precious time is essential. If you can have an opportunity fall into your lap, what could it look like?

308. Want to get to know a business owner better, but short on time and rich on good intentions?

Arrange to meet them half an hour early at a networking event or paying client meeting. That will allow you to learn what you want without interruption. And it speaks volumes about you as a business owner without impacting on the money making aspect of your day.

309. When was the last time you learnt something new?

Continual self-development is key to continued success. What could help you on your road to success?

310. More sales is not always the key to more profit. What's your expenditure like?

Are you using the best suppliers?

Getting the best rates?

Are you wasting money on unnecessary things?

311. Get emotional over your marketing. What words really hit

home to your potential customers?

Are they powerful uplifting, motivational words or are they "this would be awful, terrible without this" negative words?

Knowing what words work on your customers helps you recreate them in more of your marketing. Guess what that does to your sales and success.

312. Only networking in one place means you are only inter-acting in one place. Going regularly to more than one network-ing group ensures you are remembered by many, many business owners. Now what could THAT do for your business?

313. Action. If you concentrated on sustained action for the next week on one area in your business, what impact could it make?

What area of your business will you chose?

314. At some point you have got to ask for what you want, if you don't, who will?

If you are really nervous and struggling, practice what you will say and how you will say it.

315. Keeping things simple is good in so many ways. In public speaking, in your emails, in your marketing, in your promotions and it all adds up to a message received and understood. Are your messages simple to understand?

316. Some days you wake up and feel like anything is possible and other days you wake up feeling like it can't be done. What's different?

What do you need to do to get back into the right frame of mind?

Reframe that picture of you and see that successful fabulous busi-ness woman that I absolutely know you can be.

317. Did you know in a study of happiness, it was not the materialistic things that heightened happiness it was the sentimental ones, the people, and the simple things that money can't buy. Do you appreciate those?

And by the way, more successful people are happy people. And it starts with happiness not the other way around – that's a good one to remember.

318. When was the last time you looked at your website with fresh eyes, as if you had never seen it before?

Is it delivering quality traffic to you that you interact with effectively with?

If not is it time for a spring / autumn / winter / summer clean?

319. If you don't know how to do something, what does that mean you are agreeing to? Could that be an obstacle to your success?

320. Are you holding on to a belief that is affecting your success?

You can choose to bin negative beliefs immediately, the only one stopping you, is you.

321. Do you measure the impact of what you do in your marketing strategy? Do you measure the impact of what you are doing to achieve your goals?

If you don't measure, how can you know the impact you are truly having?

322. Question: What's the best way to interact with people on a regular basis?

Answer: Lots of ways. The more ways you interact, the higher level of success you will have.

323. Be a giver not a taker, be a healer not a fighter, be a......heck be whatever you like but be dedicated to it. And remember I believe there is such a thing as Karma. What goes around, comes around.

324. Don't sell, sell, sell with your social media. People get bored of that. They want you as the fabulous business woman that you are, interacting, chatting, sharing and giving – it all works for your business promotion, recognition and success.

325. Checking your inbox every 5 minutes will not make that email appear any faster, but it will slow down your productivity and disrupt your work flow. Have you forgotten it can take up to 35 minutes to get back into your productive flow?

326. If you really can't sleep because your mind is whizzing around with things to do. Grab a relaxing drink and write down what's on your mind. Get it out, sip that hot cuppa and let your mind clear. Don't grab the caffeine or send late night emails – how organised and under control does THAT look? If you really want to do that, schedule the email for later in the day.

327. Why is it when you are great at something you assume, that it's the same for everyone else?

And when you can't do something you assume everyone else can?

Just a thought.

328. Do you really appreciate how brilliant you are?

How talented you are?

Do you appreciate your skills that stand you apart from your competitors?

If you don't, guess what that could do for your business success?

329. Do you have the right kind of customers? Do they respect your time?

Arrive late for meetings, not return your calls, demand last minute "Can you Just"ers?

Who wants to spend all their time being unappreciated, over worked and get paid the same as they get from their lovely customers? Didn't think so – get choosy and choose the right kind of customers. It frees up your time for more success.

330. Appearance is not everything, but unfortunately did you know people have made up their mind about you within about 5 seconds of meeting you. Best to check the shoes are polished, the clothes clean and you're looking gorgeous then.

331. It's no coincidence that some people seem to find success like water in a tap. They have tapped into what success is and utilise that every day, do you? What could you do to tap into your natural path to success?

332. If you are struggling and wish you could be more like someone else, who is that person? What skills do they have?

What mannerisms?

What would they do if they were you?

Thinking like the person you most admire can really help you improve the results you are getting.

333. Never ever start a sentence with "But you won't be interested...." or "For most people this is a boring subject....." You love what you do, so be proud of it.

334. Not everything you want to achieve in your career will be difficult to do. Not everything in your career will be easy to do. But expecting things to be hard / tricky / tough how useful is that to your motivation, inspiration and success?

Expect greatness!

335. When you look in the mirror who do you see?

I imagine a successful, amazing business woman reading this, who can do it all and still have energy for a workout, a freshly cooked meal and space for me time. Well that would be nice wouldn't it?

336. Are your goals and ambitions big enough? So many business women sell themselves short, are you?

Go on aim for the moon, if you fail you will still be among the stars!

337. It's only a matter of time before someone comes along who is better than you, that's the day to give up right?

Of course not!

The highest form of flattery is replication of what you do. Shine in your brilliance, step it up a gear, and deliver even more – your customers will love you for it. Oh and never rule out collaboration.

338. Happiness is not related to where you live, how much you earn, or what you have for tea tonight. It's an internal thing that you can learn to feel even on a really bad, grotty horrible day. If you learn this skill, bad days will be easier to get through.

339. When you have done a job well done (and let's be honest that's all the time, right?) ask the happy smiley customer – who else do you know that could benefit from what I do?

Could I get their contact details?

Would you introduce me?

340. Helping those around you is a great thing to do, it gives you that warm fuzzy feeling inside and helps others soar, but don't do it at the expense of your own success. After all, you can't take that warm fuzzy feeling to the shops and exchange it for tomatoes! Sooner or later all that free stuff will grate like knees on concrete – ouch! The moral is to keep it balanced.

341. When was the last time you updated your website, blog, social media accounts?

If you don't keep things fresh, people won't stop by, and guess what?

They will be losing interest too – now that can't be good.

342. Lists are only ever any good if you are clearing things off of them. If you keep writing the same thing on your list week after week, what is THAT doing for your motivation? Need to really take action on that list ditch or deal with every item and if that doesn't work tag me in a post. Let's nail that list of things to do.

343. Know when to step away from the office and the laptop. Your brain, body and soul all need a break from work. And when you return you will find that you have the ability to be more creative, more proactive and concentrate to a higher level

344. Have you met every business woman's worst night mare?

His name is Ron.

"Later Ron" will not get it done.

So DIN – that's right, Do it NOW!

(Just wanted to check your Ron was well and truly gone!)

345. Is your website a potential customers dream or nightmare?

Do you make it obvious as to how you want them to interact?

Where are your contact details?

Your testimonials?

Your results?

Is your call to action obvious?

Do you make life easy for potential customers or make them give up?

Can people easily understand how you can help them and what results they will get?

346. Networking is a marathon not a sprint. Keep it up. Go regularly and make it count in your working day. Dedicating a little time regularly to this will provide contacts, leads and potential clients, but like the lottery says "You have got to be in it, to win it."

347. Inspiration comes in many formats. If you could bottle yours, what would that look like? Your favourite song to dance to?

A picture of your dog / partner / children / favourite destination on your fridge / desk / purse?

Where is your inspiration?

348. It's no good moaning that life is not delivering what you want if you don't do the action to get it. Right?

What DO you want?

Come on your fabulous go and get it!

349. If you were to ask your favourite customer what they

thought of you, what would they say?

If you were to ask your best friend what they thought of you what would they say?

If you were to ask me what I thought of you guess what I would say?

Do you believe that little lot?

I truly hope so.

350. Sitting at your desk solidly for 10 hours is not a sign of achievement it's a sign that your bottom is likely to ache, your eyes will be sore and your brain over worked. Spice things up a bit. Break up the day. Shake things up. Your body will love you as much as your business.

351. When was the last time you checked the numbers in your business?

No one loves number crunching (except clever people and accountants!) but every business woman should if she wants to keep an eye on her success and look at ways to grow her business.

352. Imagine you were standing next to someone that thought you were amazing. That wanted to do business with you, protect you on tough days, inspire you when your creativity disappears and motivate you to remember how fabulously brilliant you are.

I am happy to always be that person for you, who else could do that job?

Who else do you rely on?

353. There is nothing wrong with being frightened to do something new. However there is in allowing that fear to grow, take over and stop you from getting on. Tackle it today and that fear will get smaller and smaller until it disappears. Trust me, I've

seen it happen so many many times!

354. Lacking inspiration today?

Step away from the office and give that mind some space. It will thank you for it. Just 20 minutes can be enough to get the creative spark lighting up your mind. It can still be work related.

355. DPD is what you need for success. That's Dedication, Passion and Determination – And I live by it!

Do you?

356. Moaning moaning moaning, moaning, moaning moaning. Not much of a fun sentence, rather boring, monotonous and produces poor results. That's the sentence and moaning. Just saying.

357. Testimonials should not just be hidden on your Linked in profile or your website. Shout them from the rooftops!

Come on your brilliant at what you do, so spread the word and let more people get the chance to love what you do. It's not arrogance its passion for what you do.

358. Found a great resource online that other people could benefit from?

Then share it. Contrary to popular belief, instead of them relying on that and ignoring your services it actually reinforces you as the expert in your field and they will rely on you even more.

Why?

Because you are the one that they have built the relationship with, not that online resource.

359. Not all blogs need to be a page full of writing. What about a picture?

Guess how many words they are supposed to paint?

A short film – keep it short though, people can have the attention span of a small gnat.

A poem, a quote…. what would work best in your profession?

If what you do is visual a page full of writing does not necessarily allow your true brilliance to shine through. Ask yourself how best can I showcase what I do and share great ideas for people to use? You could even try asking your favourite customers since they already love what you do.

360. Everyone is always doing the best they can do. That may be a difficult statement to accept; just because it may look different to yours it does not mean it is more important or less relevant to their happiness and success. That can be important to remember when someone snaps your head off or cuts you up at the traffic lights!

361. If you don't ask, you don't get. Not everyone is going to quickly get what you are truly saying, so keep it simple and if you aren't getting what you want / need – then ask.

362. A good way to power up getting the result you want. To achieve a goal. To change a behaviour or belief that you know is limiting your success is to ask yourself this very powerful question; "If I hang on to the way I'm doing this, the belief I hold or the actions I've always taken, then what am I agreeing to?

363. That internal voice can be a right negative Moaning Minny, can't it?

"Don't do this"

"That won't work"

"Who do you think you are to get THAT!"

"You will be rubbish at that."

Guess what?

There is another version in there that is like your proud mum when you won that race/got that gold star/learnt to drive/walk/talk or sang that solo. And it can be even more powerful than Moaning Minny. Listen carefully to yours. What is it saying?

364. Life is not something that happens after 8pm and at the weekends. It can impact your success 7 days a week, 24 hours a day. If you fail to remember this. Then you are allowing yourself to meet massive obstacles at times when your priorities need to move in another direction.

365. Do you remember way back on day 11 I shared with you an idea to power up your success?

Both long term and every week?

I then reminded you about it on Day 69, Day 124, Day 179 and Day 230. So in theory you have been flying along getting tons done and getting the results you want right?

If you haven't it's because you didn't create a higher enough level of reason to act. Go back, don't berate yourself. (If it was that easy there would only be about 127 self development and business books in the world!) And concentrate on just the top item on List 1 and List 2 and nothing else. Remembering your underlining passion for achieving it at all times.

366. Never ever ever forget that you are awesome. You are capable of so much. You can reach amazing heights and smile from the top and say "Yes, I did that!"

The day you forget that, negativity will do its best to work its way in and undermine your confidence and thus attack your success. Always ensure your internal voice is as nice to you as it would be to the most important people in your life.

Now what?

So for one whole year, (if you were only reading one a day) I've been sharing with you a little golden nugget to power up your success. Have you seen results?

I know that every one of these 366 ideas works, because I've been using them on my own life and those of the business women I work with and everyone that matters to me, from best friends to even my daughter and now her friends too.

Being a confident successful business woman is within your reach. I truly believe that. Work according to your own values, check your core beliefs are working for you and look at every goal you set and ask yourself the following;

1. Do I truly accept the cause of what is preventing my success?
2. Have I taken responsibility for what was happening that was stopping me from getting the results I want?
3. Am I ready to do things differently, because if I don't I know what I would be agreeing to?
4. What is my end goal? How does it look? What does it feel like? Who would I celebrate with? Can you seriously visualise every aspect of success of that goal?
5. And lastly but most importantly what ACTION am I going to take? (And a word of caution here, if the action is not happening today, if you are finding an excuse to leave it until tomorrow you have not created a powerful enough reason to act. Action today sees results!

Success is in your reach. Confidence will radiate out from all that you do and have a great impact on your future successes.

The more you utilise this book the more success you will get. And the more success you get, will give you the experiences to believe in yourself and power you on even more to be the confident successful business woman you want to be.

I know many business women that keep this book in their car or their office or their handbags and they read it year after year reminding themselves they are very capable of achieving anything they want to and know they can turn to people like me when they need someone in their corner – because I will always be there for you.

Good Luck and keep in touch.

FURTHER MOTIVATION, SUPPORT AND IDEAS TO SUCCESS

I love hearing from readers so do feel free to get in touch. Years on I still get messages and pictures from people around the world who have read *Fight the fear – how to beat your negative mindset and win in life* sharing their life changing moments and Eureka's.

You can access all of my social media accounts via my website – www.mandieholgate.co.uk or email me at mandie@mandieholgate.co.uk

I also have courses, books and a confidential mastermind group through my organisation www.thebusinesswomansnetwork.co.uk and I share free content too on my website.

I've briefly mentioned a few of the courses and they all utilise strategies, tools and techniques I use with my coaching clients so I know they can work very powerfully so I hope they help you create similar great results too.

If you would like to know more about coaching in your workplace or on a one to one basis getting to know me through social media will help you decide if I'm right for you and I'm happy to have a chat anytime.

To sign up to my newsletter head to my site and then you can be the first to hear of new books, courses, speaking engagements and articles to power up your mind and take control.

I've always believed that everyone is capable of achieving everything they really want to and through my work I aim to prove it. You deserve the happiness and success you want so let's keep in touch and make it a reality.

www.ingramcontent.com/pod-product-compliance
Lightning Source LLC
Chambersburg PA
CBHW020603220526
45463CB00006B/2427